This book is dedicated to: My beloved Parents Late
R.S.Yadapadithaya Shishila & Late.Premalatha

KRIYA YOGA– THE ART OF SUCCESSFUL LIVING

DR SURESH KUMAR RUDRAHITHLU

Copyright © Dr Suresh Kumar Rudrahithlu
All Rights Reserved.

Contents

CHAPTER ONE

Introduction

Uddhava was the son of Devabhaga, Vasudeva's brother. Born and raised in Mathura, Uddhava was a great intellectual, educated by Brihaspati, the guru of the Devas. He was amongst the first Yadava to befriend Krishna when the latter was brought by Kamsa to Mathura from Vrindavan. In some traditions, Uddhava grew up with Krishna in Vrindavan.

The two could not be more different from each other. Uddhava was raised in the city.Krishna was raised in a village of cowherds. Uddhava was educated.Krishna was uneducated. Uddhava was a serious scholar of the scriptures.Krishna was a charming rake. Uddhava silently suffered Kamsa's excesses. Krishna overthrew Kamsa and became a rebel and hero.Though opposites, Uddhava had the wisdom to realize Krishna was no ordinary soul; he was special. And Krishna saw in Uddhava a seeker, a genuine student, not a smug academician.

Uddhava is famous for two major events. In one, he is asked to go to Vrindavan and convey to the milkmaids there that Krishna, contrary to the promise he had made, would never ever be coming back. In the other, he has to go to Dwaraka and inform everyone there that the Yadava clan has been destroyed and Krishna is dead. Both events are associated with separation, pain and death. While Uddhava is the beneficiary in the first event (Krishna comes to him), he is the victim in the other (Krishna leaves him).

When Uddhava goes to Vrindavan, the eager and anxious milkmaids mistake him for Krishna, for he comes in the same chariot that took Krishna away and as Krishna's cousin, he has similar features. But then they realize, Uddhava is no Krishna. He does not know how to comfort. He does not know how to be emotional. He is calm and composed like a priest, passing on the news with accuracy, not understanding why the women wail like children.

Uddhava advises the gopikas to read the scriptures that speak how the world is full of change and suffering and how the wise detach themselves from worldly things. The milkmaids, led by Radha lash back. This forms the basis of the famous Bhramar geet, song of the bee, where the milkmaids equate themselves with the flower that is left behind by the bee after being drained of nectar and fragrance.Krishna, the bee, has moved on to another land, to other women, to other flowers. They do not resent him or wish him to change the course of his life but they want the right to pine for him. This is viraha bhakti, devotion born of separation. Uddhava offers them knowledge to console them, but the women say, "We do not want to be consoled. Where do we put your knowledge? Every being of ours is occupied by memories of Krishna!" Uddhava the intellectual returns humbled by the unconditional love of the milkmaids. The gyan yogi understands the bhakti yogi for the first time.

Life moves on. Uddhava watches Krishna take the Yadavas out of Mathura to Dwaraka. He watches him help the Pandavas win the war against the Kauravas. In the final chapter of Krishna's life, a great civil war breaks out amongst the Yadavas. And Krishna does nothing to stop his kinsmen from killing each other. Then, a hunter's poisoned arrow strikes Krishna on the sole of his left foot. Uddhava is aghast, while Krishna calmly requests him to convey the message of his demise to the women, children and aged people, his old father included, the news of the great tragic end of the clan. "How can you be so calm?" asks Uddhava. In response,Krishna says with a smile, "Why? Are you not detached?" He then reveals to his friend the Uddhava Gita also known as the Hamsa Gita, the song of the goose.

Uddhava realizes that he is very knowledgeable but not quite wise. He knows every verse of every scripture, every argument and counter agrument, but when it comes to coping with reality he is no different from the milkmaids whose wailing he frowned upon. And unlike Radha, he does not know how to accept and let go. "If you truly have wisdom, Uddhava," saysKrishna, "you will have faith and patience."

Faith means truly accepting, material things are bound to go but not spiritual. Krishna will leave Vrindavan eventually, Krishna will leave Mathura and Dwaraka inevitably, but Vishnu's Vaikuntha will always be there. Radha knew this and so even when Krishna left and she wept, she never expected him to return physically; he was always with her emotionally. Uddhava had to still learn the lesson. Turn into a true goose, enjoy the waters but not let the water stick to his feathers. Getting Uddhava to realize this truth, not merely understand it, is the best gift anyone could offer a friend.

The instructions in the Uddhava gita bears lots of similarities to Bhagavad-gita, however, there are much more elaborations and practical analysis on how to execute the ideas that were briefly explained in the Bhagavad-gita.

Lord Krishna elaborately explained the path of self realisation, various yoga and mystic perfections, real religion, the modes of material nature and their influences, analytical understading of material nature, the process of philosophical inquiries, and the ultimate path of bhakti, which is the process of total dedication to God. In one sense, Uddhava-gita is the ultimate companion to Bhagavad-gita, as what were briefly taught in the Bhagavad-gita were now elaborately explained by the same speaker, Lord Krishna, in the Uddhava gita.

While the Bhagavad Gita is part of the Mahabharata, similarly, the Uddhava Gita occurs in the Bhagavata Purana; both epics were composed by Veda Vyasa to highlight the glory of Lord Krishnas descents into the world. There are countless translations and editions of Bhagavad-gita, and the numbers are increasing everyday. The most potent edition of Bhagavavad-gita is the edition presented by His Divine Grace A.C. Bhaktivedanta Swami Prabhupada, the founder acarya of the International Society for Krishna Consciousness. Srila Prabhupada presented Bhagavad-gita As Its, and opened the eyes of this darkened world, to the personality of Lord Krishna, which had previously being hidden by the unscrupulous and impersonal commentaries of the great book.

Lord Kṛiṣhṇa, a Vedic prince who lived about five thousand years ago, is predominantly known as the speaker of the Bhagavad Gītā, the talk He delivered to his doubting friend Arjuna just before the great battle of the Mahābhārata began. With that war the Vedic age of the great kings [Dvāpara-yuga] ended and the present age of quarrel [Kali-yuga] commenced. Ever since there was no natural relationship anymore between the sages and the rulers, for reason of which the world more or less has fallen into chaos. But there is also a second talk of Kṛiṣhṇa in which He extensively reports about His science and nature. The second time He spoke His mind to His nephew, great friend and devotee Uddhava, just before Kṛiṣhṇa left the earth. This Gītā, part of the masterly frame story the Bhāgavata Purāna - the socalled Śrīmad Bhāgavatam - is of a different tone. While He in the Bhagavad Gītā admonishes Arjuna to fight and perform his duty as a warrior, Kṛiṣhṇa in this talk advises Uddhava on how to serve Him with devotion and find liberation when He Himself is no longer physically present on earth. The story has a more personal ring, is more narrative with examples and dilates a bit more, even though sometimes the same or likewise verses are encountered. The story is therefore easier to read and less abstract.

He first of all explains to Uddhava that he has to give up his attachments in order to find liberation in His service. Without that spiritual connectedness one is a lost, eternally bound soul condemned to return again to the material world full of misery. He teaches Uddhava to recognize Him in all and everything like a thread running through a pearl necklace, as He told Arjuna. Uddhava then states, just like Arjuna again, that he finds yoga a difficult to perform discipline and asks for further instruction. Kṛiṣhṇa answers that only by one's intelligence deriving from indirect symptoms one cannot attain Him, one needs to be devoted in going for the direct symptoms of His different appearances. He proceeds to give a description about all the teachers he had. There is not one guru or source of knowledge in one's life. One learns from the earth, the air, the sea, the moth, the honey bee and many other teachers one meets.

Krishna mentions twenty-four of them in a few chapters and explains that knowledge acquired from a single teacher cannot be very solid or complete. The Absolute Truth of the complete whole is by the sages sung in many ways. Next He elaborates further on the details of His science. What would be health and what is liberation? What is the meaning of religious rituals and how must one meditate? What does perfection entail and what are His opulences? On the basis of what societal order can one be of service unto Him and what is all meant by the perfection of spiritual knowledge? Are there different forms of yoga and what would be the best one? What to say about the difference between good and evil? And how about the relation between the person and material nature?

Uddhava asks Krishna how to remain calm when one is approached with negativity by others. Krishna then relates the story of a brahmin endeavouring too frantically for material purposes and too little in respect of people. Material existence, however much one tries one's best for it, time and again results in frustrations. True happiness cannot be found that way. And thus one arrives at detachment, however lusty and prosperous one's life has been. One looks for lasting happiness after all. For that purpose one's mind must be subjected to the proper discipline of meditation. With a correct insight in matters of cause and effect one may find liberation and lasting happiness, meanwhile learning to overcome negative consequences, karmic reactions. There is no other cause of happiness and distress than the material bewilderment of one's mind. Because of that bewilderment one sees a world filled with friends and foes. One then sees Him not everywhere any longer and has lost one's way. Therefore do not judge too rashly and try to rise above the world of opposites. In transcendence one finds liberation. Kṛiṣhṇa next expounds on the nature of material reality and the degree to which we are all determined by it. Everything around us, the 5 complete of our material existence is a product of the interaction of the natural modes or qualities and functions, and the time. One has to acknowledge that there is a fourth state of consciousness next to the ones of sleeping, waking and dreamlessly being absent, an extra dimension in which one must manage to find oneself. By meditation one attains that fourth state. It is all about the stabilization of that consciousness.

Kṛiṣhṇa then relates another story. It is a story about an emperor turning into a complete fool the moment his wife abandons him. In his misery he arrives at understanding. Attached to female beauty and sense gratification a man fails to meet his essence. One therefore has to develop devotion unto Him so that a marriage does not become an unbearable burden and enjoyment is not a sin. Dedicate everything to Him, that is how one finds liberation. Kṛiṣhṇa then clarifies how one can worship His form. One organizes rituals with a material purpose and for that reason they are associated with karmic matters. But in bhakti, His devotional service, one has to learn to live one's love free from ulterior motives, especially the love for His person and wisdom. An idol is not a purpose in itself, but rather constitutes a gateway for the purpose of realizing Him from within. It is a necessary process of material actions, just as one with clocks and calendars culturally worships His impersonal nature of time until one has retrieved His original Time, nature and natural harmony.

By karma one loses oneself, by dharma one saves oneself. Karma means to suffer profit-minded labour and selflessly that is overcome. Dharma is religion and nature, and by devotion and meditation one regains that connectedness and original harmony. Kṛiṣhṇa finally offers an exposition about the interest of properly discriminating between mind and matter, between soul and body. What is actually real and what is just a denomination of that what is real? It is the identification with matter that constitutes the hindrance because of which we are locked up in a false ego of 'I' and 'mine' that we take for real.

Kṛiṣhṇa shows the way of liberation in the soul that is 6 never alone, but is always together with Him as an eternal friend, like two birds sitting in a tree. One bird enjoys the fruits, the other one is witnessing. Once being liberated one is not that much concerned any longer about all external matters so that one, self-enlightened, is elevated above the world of opposites. Kṛiṣhṇa explains how one can conquer the different hindrances in one's life and how one may attain that liberation. Appease the mind by repeating His names in silence with prayer beads, thus let go of everything and finally attain Him. Even endeavoring for one's health one must ultimately give up in order to reach His destination. Kṛiṣhṇa concludes with a discussion of the yoga of devotion, of bhakti, as the most suitable way to overcome all hindrances. He thereto pleads for seeking association with devotees, for congregational singing, for devotional service and for the beneficial effect it has on one's character. With one's devotion one should recognize Him in each and everyone and thus overcome the burden of one's mortality

CHAPTER TWO

Conversation between Lord Sri Krishna & Uddhava

<u>Conversation between Lord Sri Krishna and Uddhava:</u>

(1-3) Śrī Uddhava said: 'Oh Lord of the Universe, how many basic elements of creation [tattvas] have been enumerated by the seers? Oh Master, I heard You speak about the twenty-eight basic elements of this world . Some say there are twenty-six, others speak of twenty-five or twenty-seven, some speak of nine, some of four and others of eleven elements, while others speak of sixteen, seventeen or thirteen elements. Oh Eternal Supreme One, could You please explain to us what the sages who so differently express themselves with the calculations of their divisions have in mind with them?'

(4) The Supreme Lord said: 'With them [those elements] present everywhere the brahmins speak the way it suits them, after all, what would there for those who lifted up [the veil of] My māyā, be difficult to say?

(5) 'It is not the way you say it, it is the way I say it': this is what my unsurpassable [bewildering] energies do to

those who argue about causes .

(6) Because My energies are interacting, differences of opinion arise among the ones who talk about this subject [of causation], but when one finds peace in the control over one's senses the controversy subsides and the arguing stops [one attains the true nature of the Supreme Spirit, ātmatattva].

(7) Because the various [subtle and gross] elements mutually pervade one another, oh best among men, a speaker wants to give a fitting description with an enumeration of causes and consequences.

(8) With each of those divisions any single element refers to the other elements; whether it is there as a cause or an effect, when you see one element [like the ether] you also see all the other elements that element is part of .

(9) Discrimination as heard from the mouth of anyone who wants to reflect upon cause and effect, we accept [as authoritative], when that distinction originated from consistent reasoning.

(10) A person is stuck to eternal ignorance and cannot all by himself figure out what the process of self-realization entails. That knowledge is derived from someone else familiar with the Absolute Truth .

(11) In this knowledge concerning the good quality of material nature, there is not the slightest difference between the puruṣa - the Supreme Being, the Soul, the actual person - and īśvara the Lord. To suppose that it would be otherwise is a useless figment .

(12) The modes of goodness, passion and ignorance as the causes of [respectively] maintenance, creation and destruction, constitute material nature [prakṛti] but [do] not [control] the soul .

(13) In this world the mode of goodness is of knowledge [light], the mode of passion is of fruitive labor [karma] and the mode of ignorance is of a lack of wisdom. The interaction of the modes is called Time and that what is there by nature, the natural propensity [svabhāva], constitutes the thread [the mahat-tattva is the sūtra, .

(14) The actual person [puruṣa], material nature [prakṛti], the intelligent witnessing [mahat-tattva], the identification with the form [ahankāra], ether, air, fire, water and earth are thus the nine elements of creation I referred to [in verse 1].

(15) Hearing, touching, seeing, smelling and tasting are the five [senses] by which one acquires knowledge; the speech organ, the hands, the genitals, the anus and the legs constitute their operation, oh dear one, and the mind is there for both of them.

(16) Sounds, tactile qualities, tastes, fragrances, and forms [or colors] are the categories of the sense objects [see viṣaya] and speech, manufacturing, excretion [by anus and genitals] and locomotion are the functions covered by them.

(17) In the beginning of creation the puruṣa uninvolved witnesses the material nature of this universe, the universe that by the operation of sattva and the other modes assumes the forms of the gross manifestations and subtler causes [see also 2.10: 10].

(18) All the elements of the 'great principle' [the mahat-tattva] and what belongs to it, received their potencies from the glance of the Lord, undergo transformation and create, amalgamated by the power of nature, the egg of the universe .

(19) With the five physical elements beginning with the ether on the one hand and the individual knower [the jīva] with the Supreme Soul [the Paramātma] on the other hand, we speak of seven constituent elements as the foundation from which the body, the senses and the life air [are produced].

(20) Departing from six elements one speaks of the Transcendental Person as the sixth element conjoined with the five material elements He first projected as His creation and thereupon entered.

(21) When one speaks of four elements, fire, water and earth arise from the Original Self; from these elements this cosmos originated, the birth place of all material products.

(22) Counting seventeen there is the consideration of the five gross elements, the five senses and their five objects together with the one mind and the soul as the seventeenth element.

(23) The same way counting sixteen elements the soul is identified with the mind. With thirteen elements one has the five gross elements, the five senses, the mind and the [individual and supreme] soul.

(24) Counting eleven elements one speaks of the soul, the gross elements and the senses. With the eight natural elements [the five gross ones, mind, intelligence and false ego] and the puruṣa, the Original Person, one thereupon has nine.

(25) In this way the various divisions of the tattva elements have been contrived by the seers, all logically being supported by rational arguments; with the sages there is no lack of clarity.'

(26) Śrī Uddhava said: 'Because both nature and the enjoyer [prakṛti and puruṣa], despite being constitutionally

different, cover one another, oh Kṛṣṇa, there seems to be no difference between the two: one sees the soul within nature and nature within the soul [see also B.G. 18: 16].

(27) Please, oh Lotus eyed One, All-knowing and Very Expert in Reasoning, cut down with Your words the great doubt in my heart.

(28) The living beings receive from You the knowledge that by the potency of Your outer illusion is stolen away [again]. Only You understand the real nature of Your illusory power and no one else.

(29) The Supreme Lord said: 'Prakṛti and puruṣa [nature and the enjoyer] are completely different, oh best of all persons. This creation [prakṛti] is subjected to transformation because of the interaction of the guṇas.

(30) My dear, the deluding energy consisting of the three modes establishes by those modes a diversity of combinations and mentalities. This changeable nature based upon the guṇas is of three kinds, one is called adhyātma, the next adhidaiva and another adhibhūta .

(31) In this world one's sight [adhyātma], that what one sees [adhibhūta] and the light upon it [adhidaiva], create each other's perfection with the sun independently in the sky. [So too] the [Super]soul, the original cause separate from these three aspects, by its own conscious experience acts as the perfection of all that was achieved.

(32) Next to the eyes the same [trinity] applies to the sense of touch and what one feels with it, to the ear and what one hears, to the tongue and its occupation, to the nose with what is smelled and to one's consciousness together with its attributes.

(33) The agitation of the modes takes place on the basis of the primal ether and leads to changes [or pradhāna

constitutes the cause of the time phenomena]. The principle of the intellect [the mahat-tattva, see also ***] therefore gives rise to a false I-awareness that is the cause of three different types of bewilderment: emotion [vaikārika], ignorance [tāmasa] and sensual pleasure [aindriya].

(34) Lacking the full knowledge of the Supersoul one says things like 'this is real and that is not real' with the focus of discussion on material dualities. Although useless such [speculations] will not cease for as long as persons have turned their attention away from Me, their true abode.'

(35-36) Śrī Uddhava said: 'How do those souls whose minds are diverted from You by the fruitive activities they perform, oh Master, accept and give up higher and lower material bodies? Please Govinda explain to me what by those who are not so spiritual is not understood because they, predominantly knowing this world, were cheated.'

(37) The Supreme Lord said: 'The mind of people that is shaped by their fruitive labour, is bound to the five senses. Traveling from one world to the next, the soul, that has a separate existence, follows that 101 mind [see also linga, vāsanā and B.G. 2: 22].

(38) The mind that depending its karma always contemplates, rises because of what is seen or heard about through the senses, but inert [when dying away from the sense objects] the remembrance [of that life] is thereupon lost.

(39) This total forgetfulness of the living entity in which it does not remember a self that for this or that reason was absorbed in the objects of the senses, is what one calls death.

(40) Oh man of charity, what one calls birth is when a person completely identifies himself with the body he assumed, just like what one does in a dream or when one has a fantasy.

(41) And just as one in a dream or fantasy has no remembrance of a previous dream or fantasy, one also does not think of having had a previous existence [*4 en B.G. 4: 5].

(42) Because of the creation of this sense refuge, this body, a threefold notion [of being of a high, middle or low class birth] appears concerning the form assumed. This leads the person to [believe in] an outer duality also found inside, like giving birth to bad offspring.

(43) My best one, created bodies constantly find and lose their existence as a consequence of Time, the imperceptible, subtle energy of which one does not notice.

(44) Just like the flame of a candle, the stream of a river and the fruits of a tree, the lifespan, the circumstances and such of all created beings are determined by it.

(45) One has it wrong when one says 'this light is the same as this lamp' and 'this flow of water is the same as this river'. The same way it is wrong to say that 'this human [body] is the same as this person'. It is a way of reasoning by which men are wasting their lives

(46) Actually this person does not take birth from the seed of his own activities, nor does he die. He is immortal and was only joined [with this body] because of illusion, just like fire in firewood .

(47) Impregnation, gestation, birth, infancy, childhood, youth, middle age, old age and death are the nine stages of the body.

(48) These superior or inferior physical conditions - that one owes to one's own motives [of karmic rebirth] -,

a soul accepts as his own because of being bound to the modes, but sometimes he [by the grace of the Lord with due effort in yoga] manages to distance himself from them.

(49) From the birth of one's offspring and death of one's forefathers one may conclude to the truth [of one's own life]. He who properly understands the characteristics of this duality [and thus knows he is the continuing soul] is no longer subject to this generation and destruction of things.

(50) Someone knowing about the seed and maturity of a tree, is the witness distinct from the birth and death of that tree. In the same way one is the witness separate from the [birth and death of] the physical body.

(51) An unintelligent person who fails to distinguish between soul and matter and in touch with matter takes the external world for the real thing, lands completely bewildered in the cycle of birth and death.

(52) Wandering around because of his karma he, when he follows the mode of goodness, will go to the sages and the gods. Following the lead of passion he will move among the common people or fall into the [demoniac] grip of darkness, and by the mode of ignorance he will find himself among the ghosts and spirits or reach the animal kingdom .

(53) Observing dancing and singing persons one tends to imitate them. The same way one is, despite [as a silent witness] not being engaged, inclined towards a material intelligence when one is faced with the qualities of matter .

(54-55) Just as trees seem to move seen in water that moves and the world seems to spin when one's eyes are spinning around, one's mental impressions of experienced sense objects are neither real. Just like the things one sees in a dream are but figments of one's imagination, also the soul's image of a life of birth and death is but a phantom.

(56) For someone meditating the objects of the senses, material life will not stop despite being an illusory affair, just like the occurrence of unpleasant things in a dream.

(57) Therefore Uddhava, do not delight in the sense objects that play games with the senses. Just see how one, based upon the illusion of the material duality risen within the self, fails to realize the soul.

(58-59) When one is insulted, neglected, ridiculed or envied by bad people, or else chastised, held captive or deprived of one's means of livelihood, or when one is repeatedly spat or urinated upon by ignorant people, someone desiring the Supreme who thus being shaken is having difficulties, should save himself by resorting to his essence .

(60) Śrī Uddhava said: 'How do I learn this? Please, oh Best of All Speakers, tell us that.

(61) The offenses of ignorant people against oneself is what I find most difficult to tolerate. Even for scholars it is difficult, oh Soul of the Universe. Except for those who fixed in Your dharma in peace reside at Your lotus feet, material nature no doubt constitutes the greatest burden.' *: Two examples: A pot is part of the element earth and earth is part of a pot. All matter is part of the ether [substantial space] and ether is part of all the elements. **: The paramparā adds here: 'Śrī Chaitanya Mahāprabhu described the actual situation as acintya-bhedābheda-tattva - the supreme controller and the controlled living entities are simultaneously one and different. In the material mode of goodness the oneness is perceived. As one proceeds further, to the stage of viśuddha-sattva, or purified spiritual goodness, one finds spiritual variety within the qualitative oneness, completing one's knowledge of the Absolute

Truth' [see also siddhānta]. ***: To differentiate the basic terms used in this chapter: Prakṛti is the material nature with its living beings and guṇas, pradhāna is the primordial, undifferentiated state of matter without the specific creatures and guṇas and the mahat-tattva is the totality of the greater reality of it all, also known as the principle of intellect or the cosmic intelligence. The puruṣa is the original person who is the enjoyer: the Lord and the living beings who are the same in quality. *4: According to the well-known exception that confirms the rule says Śrīla Viśvanātha Cakravartī Ṭhākura here that by the mystic power of jāti-smara one may remember one's previous body. Patañjali in the Yoga Sutra III.18 says: 'Impressions which, carried along in the self, surface, give insight in previous states of life'. *5: The classical philosophical stance defended here is: 'When one has a body one is a soul, when one is a body one is a pig', where the pig is here the fallen soul returning time and again to a materialistic life. Chapter 18 Forbearance: the Song of the Avantī Brāhmana

(62) The son of Vyāsa said: 'After Uddhava, the greatest of the devotees, had said this to Him, the chief of the Dāśārhas whose heroism is so worthy to be discussed, He praised His servant for his words and replied.

(63) The Supreme Lord said: 'Oh disciple of Bṛhaspati, in this world there is virtually no pious soul capable of keeping his mind in check after being disturbed by the insulting words of an uncivilized person.

(64) A person is not as much hurt when pierced by arrows through a sensitive part of his body, as by the painful arrows of the harsh words of uncivilized people getting lodged in his heart.

65) In this regard Uddhava, a most pious story is told. Please listen carefully, I shall describe it to you.

(66) It was related by a mendicant who, upon being insulted by bad people, kept his composure reminding himself that it happened as a consequence of his past deeds.

(67) In Avantī [in the district of Malwa] there once lived a certain brahmin, very rich with many opulences, who earned his livelihood doing business; but he was a miserly person, full of lust, greed and very prone to anger

(68) He had no respect for his relatives and guests, not even in words, nor catered he, devoid of religiosity, at the right time to his own needs.

(69) His sons, in-laws, his wife, daughters and servants turned against the miser with his bad character and in disgust withheld their affection.

(70) Thus lacking in dharma as well as pleasure, the five claimants of sacrifice [the deities, see pañca-bhāga] became angry with that obsessive treasurer who failed for both the worlds [this and the next].

(71) By his neglect of them he lost all his credit, oh magnanimous one, and all the wealth for which he so painstakingly had troubled himself was lost.

(72) Oh Uddhava, a part of the wealth of this so-called brahmin was seized by his relatives, some by thieves, some by providence, some by time, some by common people and some by higher authorities.When he had lost his property, in him, who devoid of religiosity and pleasure was neglected by his kin, arose a hard to endure anxiety.

(73) Thus ruminating he, choked with tears, for a long time lamented in pain over his lost riches, whereupon a great feeling of disgust for worldly affairs came over him.

(74) He then said to himself: 'Alas, how painful to trouble myself that much with all this toiling for money that brought me neither pleasure, nor served the dharmic purpose.

(75) In general the wealth of misers never ever results in any happiness: in this life it leads to self-torment and when they die they end up in hell with it.

(76) However pure the reputation of the famous may be or however praiseworthy the qualities of the virtuous are, it is all destroyed with a little greed, just like what white leprosy [vitiligo] does with an enchanting, physical beauty.

(77) In the building up, realizing, increasing, protecting, spending, losing of and rejoicing with capital, man must toil, fear, worry and live with uncertainty.

(78-79) Theft, violence, lies, duplicity, lust, anger, perplexity, pride, discord, enmity, lack of faith, competition and [the three] dangers [of intoxication, promiscuity and gambling are the fifteen unwanted things known by man as the consequence of fostering riches. He who desires the ultimate benefit in life should therefore keep the undesirable, that poses as wealth, at a great distance.

(80) One's brothers, wife, parents and friends who are unified in love, all, from one moment to the next, turn into enemies over a single penny.

(81) For the smallest amount of money they agitated give in to anger, very quickly, as an adversary out for destruction, forget their goodwill and turn you down in the wink of an eye.

(82) They who do not appreciate it as a human being to have achieved a birth the immortals pray for with next to that [even] a superior second birth, destroy their self interest and head for an unfavourable destination .

(83) What person who achieved this human life, this gateway to heaven and liberation, would attach to property, a realm of meaninglessness where he is subject to death?

(84) When one does not share with the ones who deserve a share - the greater family of the gods, the seers, the forefathers, one's relatives, the living entities and oneself - one falls down like a money minded Yakṣa.

(85) What can one do as an old man when one, maddened by one's youth, strength and wealth - the means by which a smart man settles for his perfection - has wasted one's life endeavoring for money.

(86) How does [even] a man of intelligence fall victim to a never ending, vain pursuit of wealth? All the world is most bewildered enchanted by some kind of inescapable illusory power!

(87) What is the use of the goods or they who provide them, or what would be the use of the objects of desire or the people who try to satisfy you? Or, differently stated, of what use is it for someone in the grip of death to be engaged in fruitive activities that only lead to yet another birth?

(88) The Supreme Lord, the Supreme Personality who comprises all the gods and who, satisfied with me, led me to this condition of detachment, constitutes the boat for the soul [to cross the material ocean.

(89) With the time remaining [in my life] I will, free from confusion about the complete of my self-interest, restrict my body to the minimum and find perfect peace within my self .

(90) May the gods, the controllers of the three worlds with this be pleased with me. Was it not Khaṭvānga who achieved the spiritual abode in a single moment?'

(91) The Supreme Lord said: 'Thus making up his mind, the most pious brahmin from Avantī untied the knots [of desire] in his heart and became a peaceful, silent mendicant.

(92) He wandered this world alone and inconspicuous, and entered, with his self, senses and vital air under control [see tridaṇḍa], its cities and villages to subsist on charity.

(93) Seeing him as an old, dirty beggar, low-class people dishonoured him with many an insult, oh blessed soul.

(94) Some stole away his triple staff, his begging bowl, his water pot and his seat, while others took his prayer beads and his torn rags. Showing them to him they offered them back and then took them again away from the sage.

(95) When he at the river shore wanted to enjoy his share of the food he had acquired by begging, the grave sinners urinated upon it and spat on his head.

(96) He who after his vow of silence did not speak, they would challenge to speak beating him when he kept silent. Some shouted: 'This one is a thief' while others said: 'Tie him up, bind him!' and bound him in ropes.

(97) Some taunted him with disrespect like: 'This one is a religious hypocrite, a cheater who lost his wealth was thrown out by his family and has now taken to this profession.'

(98-99) 'See how this person who in his silence pursues his goal as powerful and steadfast as the king of the mountains, is as firmly determined as a [deceptive] heron.' Some ridiculed him speaking thus, while others passed foul air and, binding him in chains, kept the brahmin captive like a pet animal.

(100) Thus subjected to [the three types of] impositions as caused by other living beings, by higher powers and by

his own nature [see kleśa], he understood that whatever came his way befell him because of fate.

(101) Being insulted by lowly people trying to get the better of him he, fixed in goodness keeping firm to his duty, sang the following song .

(102) The brahmin said: 'These people are not the cause of my happiness or distress, nor can I blame the demigods, my body, the planets, my karma or the time. It is, according to the standard authorities [the śruti] nothing but the mind that causes someone to rotate in the cycle of material life.

(103) The mind acquiring the qualities of the modes becomes very strong because of them and thus gives rise to the different sorts of white [good], red [passionate] and black [ignorant] activities that lead to the conditions [the societal classes] corresponding to those colours.

(104) The uninvolved Supersoul of transcendental enlightenment as a friend exists along with - and perceives - the struggling mind, that, with the image of the world it carries, embraces the objects of desire. It is in the engagement with the modes of nature that the individual soul [bewildered by that mind] gets entangled in attachment .

(105) Charity, one's prescribed duty, niyama, yama, and listening [to the scripture], pious works and the purification by vows all entail the subduing of the mind and have as their aim the absorption of the mind [samādhi] that constitutes the supreme [self-realization] of yoga.

(106) What would be the use of caritative rituals and such for someone whose mind has been pacified by perfectly being absorbed [in Him]? Or, why would one in addition, occupy oneself with these processes of distribution and such when one has lost one's way with a

mind not under control?.

(107) Other gods [and the senses they represent] have always fallen under the control of the mind that itself never allows the control of anything [or anyone] else. He constitutes a fearsome god stronger than the strongest and the One who [in the form of His mantras] can bring him under control, is therefore the God of gods.

(108) When one [being worldly engaged] fails to subdue that difficult to conquer enemy tormenting and attacking because of its unmanageable urges, some therefore being utterly bewildered create useless quarrels and are thus with the mortals in this world friends, neuters and rivals.

(109) People whose entire mind is seized by their body, think in terms of 'I' and 'mine' and are thus blinded in their intelligence. Because of this difficult to defeat illusion of 'this I am' and 'that is someone else', they wander around in darkness. (110) When you say that [adhibhautika] another human being is the cause of your happiness or distress, you may wonder what this means for the soul; happiness and distress [thus seen] belong to the earth [and not to the soul who finds happiness by self-realization]. With whom can you be angry about the pain when your tongue happens to be bitten by your own teeth?

(111) When you [adhidaivika] say that the gods are responsible for your suffering, then how would that relate to your soul? That suffering pertains to the changeable nature [of the senses and their rulers, the soul stands apart from]. With whom should you be angry when one limb of your body hurts another limb?

(112) When you say that the soul itself [adhyātmika] would be the cause of your happiness and distress, such

a difference would be part of your own nature. But how can one when there is only the soul and nothing outside - neither happiness nor distress - blame anyone? That difference after all would be unreal then .

(113) If the planets would be the cause of one's happiness and distress, how would that relate to the soul who is unborn? The heavenly bodies relate to that what is born. A planet is only troubled by other planets so they [the astrologers] say, so with whom should the living being distinguished from his body [and his planetary positions] be angry then?

(114) If you assume karma to be the cause of your happiness and distress, what does that karma then mean to your soul? Certain is that with the animating person on the one hand and this animated body endowed with consciousness [that on itself is] not alive on the other hand, neither of both constitute the root cause of your karma. What is there left to be upset about then?.

(115) And if we say that time would be the cause of our happiness and distress, where do we find the soul in that notion? The soul is not equal to the time, the way fire is not equal to its heat and snow is not equal to [cold]. With whom must one be angry when there is no duality in the transcendental position and time quotes?

(116) For him, [the spiritual soul] superior in transcendence, there is not from anyone, from whatever side or in any way the influence of the duality [of happiness and distress], the influence of the world of opposites, as can be seen with the arising false ego [of the mind being seized] that shapes one's material existence. He who awakens to this intelligence has nothing to fear from the material creation [with all her living beings].

(117) By the worship of Mukunda's feet I will cross over the difficult to defeat ocean of material nescience. I am certain of this because of the foregoing great seers [or ācāryas] who were firmly fixed in the worship of the Supreme Soul .

(118) The Supreme Lord said: 'While he had lost his wealth and gotten detached, while he had left his home and free from moroseness traveled the earth, the sage, despite being insulted by rascals, did not forsake his duties and spoke this song.

(119) There is no other cause of happiness and grief than the bewilderment of someone's mind that in material life out of ignorance created its friends, neuters and enemies.

(120) Therefore My best, bring in every respect with an intelligence absorbed in Me the mind under control and [attain] thus being connected the essence of the science of yoga .

(121) Whoever with full attention meditates on, makes others listen or listens himself to this [song] based upon the knowledge of the Absolute as sung by the mendicant, will for certain never [again] be overwhelmed by the dualities [of happiness and grief].' *: Some think that the essence of yoga is to stop the mind all together, but Kṛiṣhṇa stresses in this chapter clearly that it is about the control, not the stopping. That stopping is an impersonalist māyāvāda buddhist technique to concentrate on one's essence and constitutes a willfully created illusion [see Buddhism]. Saying neti-neti like Prahlāda e.g. the mind will indeed concentrate on the essence which exactly will boost the mind in that direction. So with the stopping of its worldly engagement, the real engagement of the mind in

prayers and philosophy begins. Not going for the siddhis, the mystical perfections, the mind must thus be engaged for the Fortunate One, for Kṛishṇa, by means of concentration on His names, mantras and stories. By śravanam, kīrtanam etc. one has to learn to listen, sing and follow according to the scripture, the guru and the co-believers. The first two yoga sūtras & atha yogānuśānamam, yogah citta vṛtti nirodah, should be translated with 'as the lesson of yoga, now curb the rumination of the mind about worldly things' and not with 'your yoga lesson now is to stop the mind from working'. Of course one has to use one's mind, in obedience to the Holy Spirit, to the voice of God; the mind is after all an aspect of the divine ruled by Aniruddha in the catur vyūha (see also vṛtti and siddhi). Analytic Knowledge, Sāṃkhya, Summarized

(122) The Supreme Lord said: 'I shall now discuss with you the analytic knowledge as established by the classical authorities. Knowing this a person can immediately give up the bewilderment based upon the material duality.

(123) In the first age of dutifulness [Kṛta], in the beginning when there were [only] persons expert in [spiritual] discrimination, as also before that time [during the period of annihilation], the Knower was simply one and the same as the [universe] known .

(124) That One Great Undifferentiated Truth inaccessible to speech and mind [Brahman], turned into the twofold of material nature on the one hand and the enjoyment [of the enjoyer of that result] on the other hand .

(125) One essential half, material nature [prakṛti] is she [the 'mother'], who is of a dualistic nature, while he, the other entity, the knower, is called the puruṣa [the enjoying

person or male principle].

(126) By My agitation of material nature [in the form of time, of Kāla], the modes of tamas, rajas and sattva [the guṇas] have manifested in order to fulfill the desires of the living entity.

(127) From them the thread [the activating principle of the sūtra] arose, together with the principle of intelligence [mahat]. From the transformation of mahat came about the false ego [the ahankāra of the puruṣa who identifies with the object of perception] that is the cause of bewilderment.

(128) That Iawareness is thus of the three [guṇa] categories and [accordingly makes] with clarity, emotion and ignorance [alternately use of] the sense objects [tanmātra], the senses [indriyas] and the mind [manas]. Thus it [the identified self] constitutes the cause of understanding and not understanding [the so-called conscious and unconscious].

(129) The darkness of the false ego gave rise to the subtle sensations of gross matter, its emotion awakened the senses and the clarity of the identified self called for the eleven gods [see deva].

(130) Because all the elements combined to function under My influence they brought the egg of the universe into being that serves as My supreme residence .

(131) I appeared [as Nārāyaṇa] in the egg that was situated in the water of the causal ocean and from My navel a lotus arose that is known as the universe. On that lotus the self-born one found his existence [Brahmā, .

(132) He, the soul of the universe endowed with passion, created from his penance by My mercy the three different worlds called earth, the atmosphere and heaven [bhūh, bhuvah and svaha], as also its rulers [see Gāyatrī and

loka].

(133) Heaven became the residence of the demigods, the atmosphere the home of the ghostly spirits, the earthly places offered the humans and other living beings shelter and the place beyond these three is there for the Siddhas, the ones of perfection [Siddhaloka].

(134) The places of the underworld were by the master created as the residence for all asuras ['unenlightened souls' or demons] and those perfect in their ego [the 'snakes', the Nāgas]. All the destinations of the three worlds thus owe their existence to the fruitive activities proper to the modes .

(135) By penance, yoga and by forsaking [in sannyāsa] one is of the spotless destinations of mahar, janas, tapas and satya, but My destination [Vaikuṇṭha] is reached by performing devotional service.

(136) As arranged by Me, the Supporter, the Soul [the energy] of Time, one rises up from or drowns in the mighty stream of the modes of this world in which one is bound to performing fruitive labour.

(137) Whatever the small, the big, the thin and the thick of manifestation, is all brought about by the combination of material nature and its enjoyer .

(138) That what constitutes the cause of something - common matters like things of gold and things of clay - is there in the beginning, during the life as also in the end of that what was produced and is subject to transformation [and is thus illusory as for its form, compare .

(139) Something that serves as a previous ingredient of a thing that - as something different - constitutes a change of form of that ingredient, is called the true of something provided it is present from the beginning to the end

[compare .

(140) Material nature [prakṛti] the foundation of which is constituted by the causal [transformed] ingredient of the Supreme Person [the puruṣa], together with that what is the agitating agent, viz. Time [kāla], makes up the threefold of the Absolute Truth [Brahman] that I am.

(141) For as long as I look after it, the grand creation will perpetually, for the sake of the variegatedness of its qualities, generation after generation continue to exist until its dissolution.

(142) When the form of the universe that is pervaded by Me has manifested the planetary variety of its time periods [of creation, maintenance and decay], this variety with its different worlds [losing its synergy] arrives at [a dissolution into] its five composing gross elements.

(143-148) The mortal frame [at the time of annihilation] will merge with the food, the food with the grains, the grains with the earth and the earth with the fragrance. Fragrance becomes merged with the water, the water with its quality of taste, the taste with the fire and the fire with the form. Form merges with air, air merges with touch and touch merges thereupon with the ether. Ether merges with the subtle object of sound and the senses [of sound etc.] become merged with their sources [the gods of the sun and moon etc.]. The sources My dear Uddhava, merge with the mind of the ego of goodness, the controller of the sound, that dissolves in the original state of the elements [the ego of slowness]. This all-powerful primal elementary nature then merges with the cosmic intelligence [mahat]. That greater principle dissolves in its own modes and they in their turn merge with their ultimate abode, the unmanifest state of nature that merges with the infallible Time. Time merges with the individuality [the jīva] of the Supreme in command of the illusory potency and that individuality merges with Me, the Supreme Self Unborn [ātmā], who, characterized by creation and annihilation, is perfectly established in Himself and remains alone [see also.

(149) Just as with the darkness when the sun rises in the sky, how can the bewilderment of the dual mind remain in the heart of the one who seriously studies this?

(150) This is what I, the Supervisor of the Spiritual and Material world, had to say concerning this sāṅkhya instruction of analysis that breaks through the bondage of doubts of the people who both go along with and go against nature.'

(151)The Supreme Lord said: 'Oh best of persons, try to understand what I am about to say concerning the way someone is influenced by a certain mode of My material nature.

(152-155) With the mode of goodness one finds equanimity, sense control, tolerance, discrimination, penance, truthfulness, compassion, remembrance, contentment, renunciation, freedom from desire, faithfulness, modesty and pleasure within. With the mode of passion there is lust, endeavor, conceit, dissatisfaction, false pride, a desire for blessings, separatism, sense gratification, rashness, love of praise, ridicule, display of valor and hard sanctioning. With the mode of ignorance one runs into intolerance, greed, deceitfulness, violence, attention seeking, hypocrisy, listlessness, quarrel, lamentation, delusion, the suffering of depression, sloth, false expectations, fear and indolence. These, one after the other described by Me, constitute the majority of the effects of the modes. Hear now about their combinations .

(156) Oh Uddhava, the notion of 'I am this way' and 'that is a trait of mine' that people have [in relation to these qualities] when they are engaged with their mind, senses, sense objects and life breath, reflects a combination of the modes .

(157) In case a person is fixed in his religiosity, economic development and sense gratification, [also] the resultant faith, wealth and enjoyment is an expression of the interaction of the different modes.

(158) When a person in family life is of a dedication characterized by sense gratification and thereafter performs his religious duties, a combination of the modes is a fact.

(159) From someone's self-control can be deduced that he is endowed with goodness and so on, his lust is indicative of the mode of passion and such, and from his anger etcetera one may conclude that he is caught in ignorance.

(160) When someone worships Me with devotion and indifference about the results of his labour, such a person should be understood to be of a practice of goodness, whether he is a man or a woman.

(161) When one in the fulfillment of one's duties worships Me hoping for benedictions, such devotion must be understood as being of the nature of passion, and when one does it with violent intentions one is of ignorance.

(162) The modes of sattva, tamas and rajas influence the [conditioned] individual but not me; one is bound to them because they manifest in the mind and lead to attachment to life-forms and sense-objects .

(163) When the mode of goodness - which is pure, luminous and auspicious - predominates over the other two

[of passion and ignorance], a person will be blessed with happiness, religiosity, knowledge and other good qualities [see also.

(164) When passion defeats goodness and ignorance one gets attached, wants to make a difference and tends to impermanence, because of which one with profit minded actions and striving for a good name and wealth becomes unhappy .

(165) When ignorance dominates passion and goodness one's discrimination is defeated, one's consciousness is covered, one's initiative is lost and one becomes endowed with bewilderment, complaints, sleeping too much, violence and false hope.

(166) When one's consciousness clears up and the senses are no longer distracted, one achieves physical self-confidence and a detached mind; know that to be the goodness of my refuge.

(167) When the intelligence is disturbed by too much activity, when one fails to disengage from one's senses, when one is not at ease with one's body and when the mind is unsteady, you should understand that to be the symptoms of passion.

(168) Failing in the higher functions of consciousness, getting dull, being unable to focus, not being mindful, not understanding things and being gloomy you should recognize as the mode of ignorance.

(169) When goodness increases the strength of the gods increases, when passion increases the demons grow stronger and when ignorance increases Uddhava, the wild men will get on top.

(170) Know that one is wakeful in the mode of goodness, that one is sleepy in passion, that one is not aware in the ignorant mode of the living entity and that

the fourth [transcendental] state [of consciousness turīya] pervades the three .

(171) In the mode of goodness spiritual [Vedic] persons reach higher and higher, in the mode of ignorance one reaches head first lower and lower [births] and in the mode of passion one is stuck in between .

(172) Those who die in goodness go to heaven, those who die in passion go to the human world and those who die in ignorance go to hell. They however who are free from the modes come to me.

(173) Work dutifully done as a sacrifice unto me without desiring the fruits is in the mode of goodness, work done with a profit motive is of the mode of passion and work performed with violence and pressure and such, is of the mode of ignorance .

(154) Spiritual knowledge of detachment is of the mode of goodness, fostering opinions one is of the mode of passion and a materialistic conviction belongs to the mode of ignorance. Spiritual knowledge focussed upon me [however] is considered to be free from the modes.

(155) To have one's residence in the forest is of the mode of goodness, to reside in a town is said to be of the mode of passion, to reside in a gambling house is of the mode of ignorance but My residence is elevated above the modes .

(156) A worker free from attachment is of the mode of goodness, blinded by personal desire one is of the mode of passion, having lost one's memory one speaks of the mode of ignorance [but] the one who has taken shelter of me is free from the modes.

(157) In the mode of goodness one believes in spiritual matters, in the mode of passion one believes in fruitive

activities, in the mode of ignorance one is irreligious, but one is transcendental to the modes with faith in My devotional service.

(158) Food that is wholesome, pure and attained effortlessly is considered to be of the mode of goodness, [strongly] catering to the senses it is of the mode of passion and impure food that makes one suffer is of ignorance

(159) Happiness derived from the soul is of the mode of goodness, generated by sense objects it is of passion, happiness derived from delusion and depravity is of the mode of ignorance, but free from the modes happiness is found in Me.

(160) Material substance, the place, the fruit of action, time, knowledge, activity, the performer, faith, the state of consciousness and the species and destinations of life thus all belong to the three guṇas.

(161) Oh best among men, all that exists, being seen, heard or pictured in one's mind, is a composition of the three modes that was established by the unseen [Original] Enjoyer.

(162) These forms of existence [and stages of life] of the [repeatedly incarnating] living being are bound to the operation of the modes. Oh gentle one, the individual soul who, dedicated to Me in bhakti-yoga, conquers these modes that manifest themselves in the mind, qualifies for My transcendental love.

(163) They who obtained this human body by which one acquires knowledge and develops wisdom, should therefore be as smart to shake off their attachment to the modes and worship Me.

(164) A learned man should worship Me free from material association; attentively having subdued his senses

a sage should take to the mode of goodness and conquer the modes of passion and ignorance.

(165) With his intelligence pacified he, being connected [in bhakti] without any [other] dependency, should also conquer the mode of goodness. The embodied soul who [thus] freed from the modes gives up the cause of his conditioning, reaches Me.

(166) The living entity, who as an individual soul by Me thus was liberated from the modes of nature that nestled in his mind, achieves thus, by dint of the Absolute Truth, complete fulfillment and will no longer, neither internally nor externally, wander around.' *: The word nature can also be taken literally as the modes in the sense of the seasons and their primary demigods. Krishna says that Vishnu, who is the original controller above the modes, the best of the gods is of goodness , the purest mode , leading to the godliness of Him and that of the seasons He is the season of spring . As such is autumn/ spring His season of balance and of the mode of goodness. The same way the inertia of cold is representative for the mode of ignorance that is ruled by Shiva and the hyperactivity and heat of the summer is a display of the mode of passion that is ruled by Brahmā. The Song of Purūravā

(167) The Supreme Lord said: 'Having acquired this human body that is My characteristic, one achieves, being situated in My dharma, Me, the Supreme Soul of Spiritual Happiness situated in the heart.

(168) Someone who fixed in spiritual knowledge has become free from the cause of material life that is based upon the products of the modes, does not get entangled in their illusory qualities despite of being surrounded by them; although present before his eyes they are

insubstantial and nothing but illusion to him.

(169) One should never at any time seek the company of materialists devoted to the gratification of their genitals and bellies because they who follow such people will fall into the darkest pit, like a blind man following another blind man.

(170) The descendant of Ilā [called Aila or Purūravā the well-known great emperor, sang the following mighty song when he bewildered being separated from Urvaśī, in resignation managed to restrain his grief.

(171) The moment she abandoned him and left, he naked crying like a madman ran after her calling out: 'Oh my wife, oh you terrible woman, please stop!'

(172) With his mind possessed by Urvaśī he after years of insignificantly gratifying his lusts, was not satisfied and did not notice the nights coming and going.'

(173) Purūravā said: 'Just see how bewildered I got! With my consciousness contaminated by lust I, in the embrace of this goddess, did not notice my life time passing.

(174) I had no idea whether the sun was rising or setting and was, thus spending my days, alas robbed by her of countless years. (176) Oh what a pity this total bewilderment of mine because of which the body of this mighty emperor, this crown jewel of kings, became a toy animal for women!

(177) When she abandoned me, the mighty controller, together with all of my kingdom as if I were a blade of grass, I ran crying naked like a madman after the woman.

(178) Where is now the influence, strength and sovereignty of the person I am? I ran after this woman leaving me, just like an ass with the hoof being kicked for

punishment!

(179) What is the use of knowledge, austerities, renunciation, the scriptures or of solitude and silence for the one whose mind is stolen by women?

(180) To hell with the fool I am not knowing what his best interest would be; I who thought to be a scholar in achieving the position of a lord and controller but who, just like a bullock or ass, was conquered by women!

(181) For so many years serving Urvaśī's lips I, with the lust born from my mind, never got enough of the nectar, just like a fire one can never satisfy with oblations.

(182) Who else but the Innerly Satisfied Lord of the Sages, the Supreme Lord Beyond the Senses, can free someone else who lost his mind with a courtesan?

(183) Out of control with myself being dull-minded, I saw no end to my confusion, even though the goddess [Urvaśī] eloquently gave me advice .

(184) What would she have done wrong to a 'seer' like me who, taking a rope for a snake, has no notion of his real nature [his svarūpa]? I am the one out of control with his senses is it not?

(185) What does this filthy body, unclean, full of bad odors, have to offer; what are those 'pleasing [feminine] qualities' and so on anyway? They constitute an influence originating from ignorance!

(186-187) One can never tell whether this body belongs to one's parents, wife or employer, to [the funeral] fire, the dogs and jackals or to the [indwelling] soul or one's friends. One gets attached to this unholy matter and praises it, in case of a woman, for having such a cute nose, beautiful smile and face, but one heads with it for the lowest destination [of decay].

(188) In what sense would one differ from worms when one enjoys that what is composed of skin, flesh, blood, muscle, fat, marrow and bone, urine, stool and pus?

(189) A man understanding what's best for him, should never run after women or associate with men thus engaged, for the sole reason that the mind united with the senses reaches for sense objects and thus gets agitated .

(190) [Because] a thing not heard or seen gives no rise to mental agitation, the mind of someone not engaging his senses becomes fixed and pacified.

(191) When not even wise men can rely on the six enemies [lust, anger, greed, bewilderment, intoxication and envy; the ṣaṭ-varga], then what about persons like me? One therefore should not get sensorily attached to women or to men attached to women .

(192) The Supreme Lord said: 'He, the worshipable lord of gods and men, who thus sang his song [of complaint], then gave up the world of Urvaśi. Realizing Me, the Supersoul in his heart, he with the transcendental knowledge found peace within himself and ended his illusion.

(193) An intelligent person having abandoned bad association therefore should be fixed on devotees, for only by their words he can cut off the deep attachment of his mind.

(194) Devotees with their minds fixed on Me do not depend [on lusts] and are, with an equal minded vision, completely peaceful and free from possessiveness, false ego, the dualities and greed.

(195) Oh most fortunate one, these greatly fortunate souls are constantly discussing My stories that have the power to completely eradicate the sins of anyone who

chooses for them.

(196) They who, faithfully dedicated to Me, hear, chant and respectfully take them [My stories] to heart, will attain My bhakti.

(197) What else would there remain [to be accomplished] for a devotee once he has achieved devotional service unto Me, the One of Countless Qualities who is the Absolute Truth comprising the experience of spiritual happiness?

(198) Just as cold, fear and darkness will dissipate for the one who resorts to the supreme grace of fire [Agni], similarly dullness, apprehension and ignorance will dissolve for someone who serves the devotees.

(199) For those who submerge and again rise in the fearful ocean of material life, the saintly devotees, peaceful in understanding the Absolute, constitute a supreme shelter as good as a life boat for people drowning in the water.

(200) Devotees constitute the refuge of those afraid to fall down, as good as food is there to grant the living beings their life, I exist as the shelter for the distressed and dharma is there as the wealth of the deceased.

(201) The devotees grant you the [divine] eyes while the sun [only] shows the external world after having risen; they are the worshipable ones, one's [true] relatives, they are one's actual self and Me as well .

(202) He [Purūravā] who for that reason no longer desired the world of Urvaśī, then liberated from all attachment, innerly satisfied wandered this earth On Respecting the Form of the Lord Śrī Uddhava said: 'Can You please explain the ritual yoga [kriyā-yoga] of the service unto You as a deity, oh Master? Who is of that worship, in respect of what form is one of worship and in what

manner are You worshiped then, oh Master of the Sātvatas [see also mūrti and The sages Nārada, Bhagavān Vyāsa and my preceptor the son of Angirā [Bṛhaspati] repeatedly say that for the welfare of men there is nothing as conducive. The words about this that emanated from Your lotus mouth were spoken by the great unborn Lord [Brahmā] unto his sons headed by Bhṛugu and by the great Lord Śhiva speaking to the goddess Pārvatī, . This [service to Your deity form] is approved by all classes and spiritual orders of society and is, I think, most beneficial for women and the working class, oh Magnanimous One. Oh Lotus-eyed Lord, please, oh Controller of All Controllers in the Universe, speak to Your bhakta - who is so very attached - about this means of liberation from the bondage of karma.'

(203) The Supreme Lord said: 'The number of [karma-kānda] prescriptions for worshiping deities is endless Uddhava, let Me in brief explain it nicely one step at a time.

(204) One should worship Me as one desires following one of the three kinds of sacrifice according to the Vedas, the explanatory literatures [tantras like the Pañcarātra] or a combination of them.

(205) Now hear from Me how a person, who according to the for him specific Vedic precepts [*] achieved the status of a second birth, should worship Me with faith and devotion.

(206) He must, connected in bhakti, free from ulterior motives ['honestly'] with the necessary paraphernalia worship Me, his worshipable guru, as being present in a deity, a sacrificial area, a fire, in the [position of the] sun, in water or in the twice-born heart itself [**].

(207) For purification he should first bathe and brush his teeth and next purify himself with both types of [Vedic

and tantric] mantras while applying clay and such.

(208) To be freed from his karma, he perfectly convinced should engage in My ritual worship [pūjā] and thereto perform duties as prescribed in the Vedas with worship and such [like expressing the Gāyatrī-mantra] at the three junctures of the day [dawn, noon and sunset].

(209) There are eight types of forms with which one remembers Me: in stone, wood, metal, smearable substances [like clay], being painted, in sand, in jewels and as an image kept in the mind.

(210) Of the two kinds of individual temple deities that are moved and not moved, the installed deity, oh Uddhava, is in His worship not brought forward (āvādana) and taken away again (udvāsa).

(211) Not being installed one has these options, but when assigned a fixed place the following two possibilities are found: not being of a smearable substance [or being painted or made of wood] He is washed, in all other cases He is cleansed without water.

(212) There is the worship of My different deities with excellent paraphernalia, there is the worship of a devotee free from material desire using whatever that is readily available and there is the worship in the heart in a mental respect [by love only].

(213-214) With a deity [in the temple] customary bathing and decorating is most appreciated Uddhava, for a holy place that is an exercise of respect in mantras [tattva-vinyāsa] and for fire oblations [of sesame, barley etc.] drenched in ghee are considered best. With the sun that is a meditation in āsanas [see Sūrya-namskar] and with water offerings of water and such are most suitable. Offerings presented with faith by a devotee of Mine are most dear to

Me, even if it is just a bit of water.

(215) And what to say of an offering [by devotees] of foodstuffs, flowers, lamps, fragrances and incense ? An offer [by contrast] that, even if it is very rich, is made by a non-devotee will not satisfy Me .

(216) Cleansed, having collected the necessary items, having arranged the seat with blades [of kuśa grass] pointing to the east and sitting down facing the east or the north or else directly facing the deity, he should then be of worship.

(217) After having assigned mantras to his own body and also having done this to My form, he should clean My Deity with his hand and properly prepare the sprinkling vessel and the sacred pot.

(218) With the water of the vessel sprinkling the area of the deity, the utensils and his own body, he next should prepare three vessels with water and arrange for the necessary auspicious items as far as available [like flowers, grains, blades of grass, sesame seeds etc.

(219) With the mantras for the heart [hṛdayāya namah], the head [śīrase svāhā] and the tuft of hair [śikhāyai vaṣaṭ] the worshiper should purify the three vessels of water for His feet [pādya], His hands [arghya], and His mouth [ācamana], and do the same with the Gāyatrī.

(220) He should meditate on the Original Individuality of all Expansions, the very subtle transcendental form of Mine that, within his body that was fully purified by air and fire, is situated on the lotus of the heart and by perfected souls is experienced in the end vibration of the Praṇava .

(221) With that [meditated form] by his own realization conceived, he, of worship within his body and fully being absorbed in thought of Me, should invite Me within the

deity - and all that is respected along with it - by touching My limbs with mantras [nyāsa] and thereupon honor Me [externally by performing puja].

(222-223) After first having imagined My seat decorated with the nine śaktis and the [deities of] dharma etc. [*4] as an effulgent eight-petaled lotus with saffron filaments in its whorl, he should offer to Me the pādya, arghya and ācamana water and other items of worship to be perfect with the two [of enjoyment and liberation] in respect of both the Vedas and the tantras.

(224) One after the other he next must honor My discweapon [the Sudarśhana chakra], conch [the Pāñcajanya], club [the Kaumodaki] and arrows and bow [the Śarnga], My [Balarāma items of the] plow and pestle [hala and muṣala], My gem [the Kaustubha], garland [the Vaijayantī] and chest mark curl of white hairs [the Śrīvatsa].

(225) [He also honors] Garuda, Nanda, Sunanda, Pracanda and Canda, Mahābala, Bala, Kumuda and Kumudekṣaṇa [My carrier bird and eight associates].

(226) Durgā, Vināyaka [Ganeśa], Vyāsa, Viṣvakṣena the spiritual masters and the demigods - each in their own place facing the deity - should be worshiped with the sprinkling of water and other rituals .

(227-228) Every day [the deity] should be bathed, as far as the means permit, using different kinds of water scented with sandalwood, uśīra root, camphor, kunkuma and aguru. Also hymns should be chanted such as the ones from a section of the Vedas known as Svarna-gharma, the incantation called Mahāpuruṣa, the Puruṣa-sūkta [from the Ṛg Veda] and songs from the Sāma Veda like the Rājana and others.

(229) My devotee should lovingly decorate Me with clothing, a sacred thread, ornaments, marks of tilaka, garlands and [apply] fragrant oils, the way it is enjoined.

(230) The worshiper should with faith present to Me pādya and ācamana water, fragrances and flowers, whole grains, incense, lamps and other items.

(231) According to his means he should make offerings of foodstuffs like candy, sweet rice, ghee, rice flour cake [śaṣkulī], sweet cakes [āpūpa], sweet rice flour dumplings with coconut [modaka], spicy sweet wheat cake of ghee and milk [samyāva], yogurt and vegetable soups.

(232) On special days or else every day [the deity] should be offered a massage with ointment, a mirror, an eucalyptus stick for cleaning the teeth, a bath, food to be chewed and not to be chewed, as also song and dance.

(233) In a sacrificial area set up as prescribed he should, wearing a girdle, using a fire pit and an elevation for sacrificing, by hand build and bring to a blaze a fire that is equally piled up.

(234) Spreading [kuśa grass, mats] and then sprinkling and ceremonially [anvādhāna] placing wood in the fire according to the rules, he should, having arranged for the ācamana water, sprinkle the items to offer and meditate on Me as residing in the fire.

(235-239) Meditating in worship of Me as being brilliant with a color of molten gold, with My conch, disc, club and lotus, My four arms and peacefulness; My garment with the colour of the filaments of a lotus, shining helmet, bracelets, belt, the ornaments on My arms, the Śrīvatsa on My chest, the effulgent Kaustubha and a flower garland; throwing pieces of wood soaked in ghee into the fire and in the course of the arghya ritual making the two offerings of sprinkling ghee [in two ways called Âghāras] and [two different] oblations of ghee [called Âjyabhāgas], a learned person should, with root mantras and the [sixteen lines of the] Puruṣa-sūkta hymn, offer the oblations into the fire for Yamarāja and the other demigods called Swiṣṭikṛt in due order using a mantra for each

(240) Thus having been of worship he should bow to offer obeisances unto My associates and next present offerings chanting the basic mantra for the deity in question, thereby remembering Nārāyaṇa as the Original Self of the Absolute Truth.

(241) After having offered ācamana water and giving the remnants of the food to Viṣvakṣena, he should present to Me prepared betel nut with fragrant substances for the mouth.

(242) He should [next] for some time become absorbed in celebration by listening himself and make others listen to My stories, by acting out My transcendental activities and by dancing, chanting loudly and singing along with others.

(243) With prayers from the Purāṇas, with large or small prayers from other ancient scriptures, with prayers written by others [see bhajans] and prayers from more common sources, he should prostrate himself, pay his obeisances and say: 'Oh Lord, please show Your mercy [prasīda bhagavan].'

(244) Placing his head at My feet with his palms brought together [he may say a prayer like:] 'Oh Lord, please protect this surrendered soul who in this material ocean is afraid of being devoured by death [prapannam pāhi mām īśa, bhītam mṛtyu-grahārnavat.

(245) Praying thus he should put the remnants granted by Me to his head and do this prayer once more - when the

deity respectfully is to be bidden farewell - to give the light [of the deity] a place within the light .

(246) Whenever one develops faith in Me, in whatever deity form or other manifestation, one should for that form be of worship since I, the Original Soul of All, am situated within My own form as also in all living beings.

(247) By thus being of worship with the [ritual] processes of acting in yoga as described in the Vedas and more specialized texts, a person will, in both this life and the next, by My grace achieve the perfection he desired.

(248) In order to properly establish My deity the devotee should build a strong temple and maintain beautiful flower gardens [that provide flowers] for daily pūjā, festivals and yearly occasions.

(249) In order to assure the continuance of the daily worship and the special occasions, he donates land, shops, cities and villages and will achieve an opulence equal to Mine.

(250) Installing a deity one attains the entire earth, building a temple one attains the three worlds and performing pūjā and likewise services one attains the realm of Brahmā, but when one does all of these three one will attain a quality [a transcendental integrity] equal to Mine.

(251) He who free from ulterior motives worships Me thus, will by bhakti-yoga unite his consciousness in devotion and attain Me .

(252) The one who destroys [or steals away] the service [and/or the goods] delivered to the gods and the brahmins by oneself or by others, is a stool-eating worm bound to take birth for a hundred million years .

(253) The perpetrator [of that kind of offense] as also his accomplice, the one who instigated it and the one who

approved it, all will have to share the karmic consequences in the life that follows over and over [depending the degree of the damage done].' *: The paramparā says to this that members of the three higher classes of society all achieve the twice-born status by initiation into the Gāyatrī mantra. Brāhmana boys may according to the tradition after due preparation be initiated at the age of eight, kṣhatriya boys when they are eleven and vaiśya boys at the age of twelve. **: The materialistic devotee - almost any person thus - is of devotion with the help of an image of God in the form of a timetable, the sacrificial ground in the form of the desk in his office, the fire in the stove on which he regularly cooks his meals, the sun with the date on the solar calendar and the clock he is manipulating pragmatically, the water with the daily shower he takes and the dishes he washes, and with the twice-born heart that he in his daily contemplations according to the wisdom as an adult acquired from personal experience and from his teachers. Everyone is thus, more or less engaged in devotional service in the practices of devotion as mentioned here, be it at an unconscious materialist and rather impersonal level (see prākṛta). 'Śrīla Śrīdhara Svāmī gives references from the Vedic literature stating that the water meant for bathing the feet should be combined with millet seeds, dūrvā grass mixed in water, Viṣṇukrānta flowers and other items. The water used for arghya should include the following eight items - fragrant oil, flowers, unbroken barleycorns, husked barleycorns, the tips of kuśa grass, sesame seeds, mustard seeds and dūrvā grass. The water for sipping should include jasmine flowers, ground cloves and kakkola berries' .The seat of dharma is imagined here as consisting of righteousness, wisdom, detachment and supremacy for its legs, the opposite values for the sides of the seat and the three guṇas for the three planks of the base. *5: According to Śrīla Jīva Gosvāmī the personalities mentioned here are eternally liberated associates of the Lord who reside in the spiritual sky beyond the material manifestation. Not so much the Ganeśha who in this world, as the son of Lord Śhiva, is famous for awarding financial success, and the goddess Durgā, the wife of Lord Śhiva, renown as the external, illusory potency of the Supreme Lord. Devotees accepting flowers, food or fire from the deity customarily take the offering first to their head as a token of respect. The paramparā adds here: 'By regulated, faithful worship one gradually understands that the deity is completely nondifferent from the Supreme Lord Himself. At that stage one, on the strength of deity worship, rises to the second-class platform of devotional service. At this more developed stage one desires to make friendship with other devotees of the Lord, and as one becomes solidly established in the community of Vaiṣṇavas, one completely gives up material life and gradually becomes perfect in Kṛiṣhṇa consciousness' Jñāna Yoga or the Denomination and the Real The Supreme Lord said: 'When one understands that the world, this combination of matter and person, is based upon one and the same reality, one should refrain from praising and criticizing someone else's nature and activities.

(254) He who praises or criticizes someone else's nature and actions quickly looses grip on that what is his own interest because he gets entangled in a self-created reality.

(255) A person aware of the objective diversity is just [as unaware of the one reality] as an embodied soul whose

senses overcome by sleep within the physical encasement experience the illusory [of a dream] or the deathlike of having lost consciousness.

(256) How can one distinguish between good and bad with this material duality that belongs to the realm of our imagination? Musing over it with our mind and expressing it in words we do not cover the truth [*].

(257) Shadows, echoes and mirages, though mere projections, create motives [in people]; the same way the body and all of its material conceptions create fear until the day one dies.

(258-259) The Supreme Soul who alone creates the universe and is created as its Lord, protects and is protected as the Self of all Creation and withdraws and is withdrawn as the Controller. Accordingly no other entity can be ascertained as existing apart from Him, and thus has this threefold appearance established within the Supreme Self and consisting of the modes no [other or independent] basis; know that the threefold [of the seen, the seeing and the seer according to respectively the tamas, the rajas and the sattva quality] is a construct of the illusory energy [under the influence of Him in the form of Time].

(260) Someone who fixed in the knowledge as laid down and realized by Me knows about this, does not blame or praise [in looking for another cause], he freely wanders the earth just like the sun does.

(261) When one from direct perception, logical deduction, scriptural truth and one's self-realization knows that the inessential has a beginning and an end, one should move around in this world free from attachment

(262) Śrī Uddhava said: 'O my Lord, who is it actually who carries the experience of this [changing] material

existence? It is not precisely the [unchanging] soul, the seer who is self-aware, nor does it belong to the body, the seen that [changing itself] has no experiencing self of its own.

(263) The inexhaustible soul, free from the modes, is pure, selfluminous and uncovered just like a fire, while the material body is like firewood that is without understanding. To which of the two belongs the experience of a material life in this world?'

(264) The Supreme Lord said: 'As long as the soul is attracted to the body, the senses and the vital force, his material existence, which carries its fruit in due course, will nevertheless be meaningless because of a lack of discrimination.

(265) Even though material substance has no real existence [because of its impermanence], the material condition [as for its constituent elements] does not cease to be and one has, like in a dream contemplating the objects of the senses, to face the consequent disadvantages.

(266) That [dream] what brings the one who is not awake in his sleep many undesirable experiences, will certainly not confound the one who awakened though.

(267) Lamentation, elation, fear, anger, greed, confusion, hankering and such is seen upon the birth and death of one's identification with the body [ahankāra] and does not depend on the soul.

(268) Falsely motivated dwelling within the self of the material body, the senses, life-air and the mind, the living being assumes his form according to the guṇas and the karma. He is then, depending the way he relates to the thread constituted by the greater of nature, described with different names when he under the strict control of Time

wanders about in the ocean of matter.

(269) This without a firm basis being represented in the many forms of the mind, the speech, the life force, the gross body and fruitive actions, will, with the sword of transcendental knowledge that was sharpened in worship, be cut down by a sober sage who walks the earth free from desires.

(270) Spiritual knowledge [entails] the discrimination [of spirit and matter and is nourished by], scripture and penance, personal experience, historical accounts and logical inference. [It is based upon] that which is there equally in the beginning and in the end of this [creation] and which is the same in between, knowing the Time and Ultimate Cause [of brahman, the Absolute Truth.

(271) Like gold alone being present before it is processed, when it is processed and in the final product of the processing, I am present in the disguise of the different modes [of processing] of this creation.

(272) My dearest, this spirit of condensed knowledge in its three conditions [of wakefulness, sleep and unconscious sleep], constitutes, manifesting itself in the form of the modes as the causing [of rajas], the caused [of tamas] and the causer the fourth factor [the 'gold'] which as an independent variable stands for the single truth of each of them.

(273) That what was absent before, is absent afterwards, and isn't there [independently] in between, is but a designation; whatever that was created and is known by something else, is actually only that something else; that is how I see it.

(274) The spiritual reality of God as established in its own light manifests the Absolute Truth as the variety of the senses, their objects, the mind and the transformations.

For that reason is this creation, that because of the mode of rajas is subject to modification, self-luminous, even though it is not really there [see also siddhānta].

(275) When one this way by discriminating logic has achieved clarity about the Absolute of the Spiritual Truth, one must expertly speak against and cut with the doubt regarding the Self and satisfied in one's own spiritual happiness desist from all lusty .

(276) The body made of earth is not the true self, nor are the senses, their gods or the life air, the external air, water, fire or a mind only interested in food; nor are the intelligence, material consciousness, the I that thinks itself the doer, the ether, the earth, material things or the restraint.

(277) What's the merit of him who properly ascertained my identity and in his concentration managed to direct his - by the modes controlled - senses perfectly? And what on the other hand would be the blame for him who is diverted by his senses? Would the sun care about being covered by clouds or a sky clearing up?

(278) Just as the sky is affected by the coming and going qualities of the air, fire, water and earth or by the qualities of the seasons [of heat and cold], is likewise the Imperishable Supreme elevated above the influence of the natural modes of sattva, rajas and tamas that are responsible for the fact that he who takes his body for the true self is caught in the material worl.

(279) Nevertheless, until by firmly being rooted in My bhakti-yoga one has banned the impurity of the mind of passion, one must eliminate the attachment associated with the qualities that belong to the deluding material energy

(280) The same way as a disease that was imperfectly treated turns back time and again and brings a man trouble, the mind that was not purified of its contamination of karma will torment the imperfect yogi who [still] is of all kinds of attachments.

(281) Imperfect yogis who are commanded by impediments in the form of the human beings [family members, disciples etc.sent by the thirty gods [see tridaśa] will, on the strength of their perseverance in their previous life once more [in a new life] engage in the practice of yoga, but never again be entangled in fruitive labour .

(282) A normal living being who has to experience the consequences of his fruitive labour, remains, impelled by this or that impulse, in that position until the moment he dies. But someone intelligent is, despite being situated in the material position, not that [fickle], because he with the experience of the happiness he found gave up his material desire.

(283) He whose consciousness is fixed in the true self doesn't give it a moment's thought whether he is standing, sitting, walking or lying down, urinating, eating food or doing whatever else that manifests from his conditioned nature.

(284) Someone intelligent doesn't take anything else for essential. Whenever he sees the not really [independently] existing things of the senses, he from his logic denies them their separateness, so that they are like the things of a dream that lose their value when one wakes up.

(285) Material ignorance which under the influence of the modes of nature assumes many forms is by the conditioned soul taken for an inextricable part of himself, but the ignorance ends by simply developing His vision, My

best one. The soul on the other hand is not something one accepts or leaves behind.

(286) When the sun rises is the darkness in the human eye expelled, but that rising is not creating the things that are seen then. Similarly a thorough and adroit search for the true of Me puts an end to the darkness of someone's intelligence [while that search itself is not the reason why his soul exists].

(287) This selfluminous, unborn, immeasurable Greatness of Understanding who is aware of everything is the One Without a Second in whom words find their closure, and by whom impelled the speech and the life airs move.

(288) Whatever the notion of duality the self might have is but a delusion to the unique soul, as it indeed has no basis outside of that very self .

(289) The dualistic, imaginative interpretation [in terms of good and bad by socalled scholars of this in names and forms perceivable duality which unmistakably consists of the five elements, is in vain].

(290) The body of the yogi who with a lack of experience tries to engage in the practice of yoga, may be overcome by rising disturbances. In that case is the following the prescribed rule of conduct:

(291) Some disturbances may be overcome by postures [āsanas] combined with concentration [dhāranā], penance [tapas, see ***], mantras and medicinal herbs.

(292) Some of the inauspicious matters can be overcome step by step by constantly thinking of Me [Viṣṇu-smarana], by the celebration of My names and such [japa, saṁkīrtana] and by following in the footsteps of the masters of yoga .

(293) Some [yogis] make their self-controlled bodies suitable by fixing themselves on the youthful with the help of various methods and try that way to be perfect in their material control [siddhis].

(294) By the ones who enjoy a good condition that is not honored though, convinced as they are that such an endeavor is quite useless, because the body, like the fruit of a tree, will perish anyway .

(295) Someone with a devoted mind does not value it highly to practice yoga regularly with the purpose of realizing a healthy body, he who is devoted to Me gives up on the yoga [for that purpose, *4].

(296) The yogi following this process of yoga will, freed from desires having taken to the shelter of Me, not be disheartened by obstacles and [thus] experience the happiness of his soul.' *: Contrary to popular notions that the medium would be the message, here is stated clearly that the medium is not the message. The words and the ideas, and also the so-called fixed form of things, are all false relative to the original truth, the message, the essence. That what is expressed is the essence, not the expression itself. So the one living being of the person and the living material nature with her Time as the masculine aspect, is the essence and all ideas, fixed things of it and words about it are actually false. Thus we have the paradox of the in itself false expression in words and ideas, this sentence before you as a reader e.g., of that what is true on itself as the wholeness of life. So there are idols of Kṛiṣhṇa being worshiped with the strict warning not to consider them as something material. Thus praise and criticism, good and bad, are dual notions missing the point of what is objectively the value free reality of brahman, the Absolute

Truth of the reality free from illusion that is equally present both outside and inside. Or as one puts it these days: science is value-free. **: The purport of this is that, even though material nature as His gigantic virāṭ-rūpa form is nondifferent from the Supreme Lord (as elaborately described in this and other chapters), one who has yet to conquer material desire must not artificially seek solace in material things, declaring them to be nondifferent from the Lord . Concerning penance the beginner is reminded of the fact that voluntary penance, voluntary suffering, is better than penance enforced from the outside in the form of a disease, legal prosecution, shortage, calamities etc. Like the Jews in Exodus would be ready to leave Egypt one should be ready for the coming of the Lord . Here one is reminded of the fact that characters like Rāvana and Hiranyakaśipu also practiced yoga and attained fitness; attaining perfections that way can also be something demoniac and is thus not the object of belief as stated here. Attaining the Lord is rather the motive for the yogi. Control, health and order is something nice to achieve

Bhakti Yoga: the Most Auspicious way to Conquer Death

(297) Śrī Uddhava said: 'This process of yoga is, I think, most difficult to execute for someone not spiritual. Please, oh Acyuta, tell me in simple terms how a person may easily succeed .

(298) Generally, oh Lotus-eyed One, [beginning] yoga practitioners get frustrated trying to unite the mind and, unable to find absorption, grow weary of subduing their thoughts.

(299) For that reason, oh Lotus-eyed Lord of the Universe, the swanlike [devotees] delight in taking to the shelter of Your lotus feet that are the source of all ecstasy,

while they who take pride in the results of their yoga, do not [take shelter] and are defeated by Your material energy.

(300) It comes as no surprise Achyuta, that You as a friend to all servants with no other shelter, are joined in intimacy with them [are commanded by them], You who [as Rāma] were affectionate with the animal-like [Vānaras] while the edges of Your footstool were covered by the effulgent helmets of the great controllers [like Brahmā].

(301) Knowing the benefit You offer, oh Supreme Soul, Bestower of All Perfections and dearest Lord to those seeking shelter, who would reject You or ever be devoted to anything else and forget [about You in exchange] for some opulence? What would not be granted to us when we serve the dust of Your feet.

(302) The scholars - despite all their work - would not even with a lifetime as long as Brahmā's be capable of expressing the gratitude [we owe You], oh Lord. For You, in order to remind us of the greater [spiritual] joy for dispelling the sadness of being embodied, show us Your path in two ways: in the form of that what from the caittya authority [of the Supersoul] is mentally conceived within and that what from the outside is conceived on the authority of the ācārya [the paramparāguru of the tradition].'

(303) Śrī Śuka said: 'Thus questioned by Uddhava who in his heart was most attached to Him, the Lord of all Lords spoke lovingly with an attractive smile, He who - with the universe as His plaything - by His energies assumed His three [principal] forms [the guṇaavatāras].'

(304) The Supreme Lord said: 'I shall explain to you My most auspicious dharma by means of which, with faith executed, a mortal being may defeat unconquerable death.

(305) He whose mind is attracted to My devotional service and has offered his heart and intelligence unto Me, should remember to perform step by step all his prescribed duties for My sake.

(306) One should take shelter of the holy places frequented by My saintly devotees and [follow the example of] the conduct of My devotees among the demigods, humans and demons.

(307) Either alone or in association one should with respect for the position of the moon [e.g.], at special occasions and at festivals engage in singing and dancing and so on, with royal opulence [and generous contributions].

(308) With a pure heart one should see Me, the Supreme Soul free as the sky, as being present within and without oneself and all living beings .

(309-310) Oh brightest spirit, when one with My love thus is of respect for all living beings, one with such an approach has taken shelter of the highest possible knowledge, the absolute unity of spirit. This way regarding the brahmin and the outcast, the thief and the man faithful to the brahminical culture, the sun and the spark, the gentle one and the cruel one equally, one is considered a wise person .

(311) Of the person who constantly meditates upon My presence in all men quickly the rivalry, envy, disdain and false ego will disappear.

(312) Ignoring the laughter of one's friends and without being embarrassed about outer appearances one should [factually] throw oneself like a rod to the ground and offer one's obeisances to [all,] even [to] dogs, outcasts, cows and asses.

(313) With the functions of what one says, thinks and does, one this way will have to be of worship as long as

one has not developed the vision of Me being present in all living beings [see also tridaṇḍa].

(314) For the one who by knowledge and realization sees the Supreme Soul everywhere, everything is based upon the Absolute Truth. Thus free from doubt he should desists from material striving.

(315) I consider this - with the functions of one's mind, words and actions seeing Me within all living beings - the most appropriate of all processes.

(316) My dear, because this by Me perfectly established method is free from the modes and has no ulterior motives there is, when one thus tries to be of service unto Me Uddhava, not even the slightest loss .

(317) Oh best among the pious souls, when one is capable of performing one's duty free from ulterior motives for the sake of Me, the One Supreme, [the emotions] of that endeavour like fear and such, will be futile.

(318) This in one's life by means of the false and mortal achieving of Me, the One Immortal, constitutes the cleverness of the clever and the intelligence of the intelligent.

(319) This survey both in brief and in detail I thus explained to you, constitutes the complete science of the Absolute Truth that even for the demigods is difficult to access.

(320) With clear, logical arguments I repeatedly explained to you the spiritual knowledge; properly understood this will put an end to the doubts a person may have and liberate him.

(322) He who concentrates on this question of yours as also on My clear reply, will attain the eternal secret of the Vedas, the Supreme, Absolute Truth.

(323) I shall naturally, give Myself to that person who without reservation passes on to devotees this traditional instruction of Mine, this knowledge of the Absolute Truth.

(324) He who repeats [for others] this Supreme [Knowledge] that is so sanctifying and clear, reveals My presence with the lamp of knowledge and will find purification day after day.

(325) The person who attentively and with faith regularly listens to this and is of transcendental devotional service unto Me [is a bhakta], will not get entangled in karmic activities.

(326) Uddhava, oh friend, do you have a clear understanding of the spiritual now and has this lamentation and illusion that arose in your mind been removed.

(327) Do not share this with a hypocrite, an atheist or a cheat, nor with someone not willing to listen, a non-devotee or an obstinate person.

(328) Share it with a person free from these bad qualities, someone virtuous and pure, kindly disposed and dedicated to the welfare of the brahmins, as also with labourers and women if they are of devotion .

(329) For the inquisitive one fully understanding this, there is nothing further to know; once one has drunk the nectar of this palatable beverage nothing will remain.

(330) Everything that people of success with the four goals of life [catuh-vidah] may find in knowledge, fruitive labour, mystic yoga, ordinary activities or in political ruling, you can equally find in Me My best one .

(331) When a mortal surrenders himself to Me and forsakes all his fruitive labor in his desire of service, he at that time attains freedom from birth and death and qualifies for sharing in My nature.'

(332) Śrī Śuka said: 'After he had heard the words of Uttamaśloka and thus was shown the path of yoga, Uddhava with folded hands said nothing because his throat was choked up with love and his eyes were brimming with tears. (36) Checking himself to steady his mind that was overwhelmed by love, oh King, he felt most grateful. With folded hands he touched the lotus feet of the Hero of the Yadus with his head and addressed Him.

(333) Śrī Uddhava said: 'The great darkness of the delusion I embraced, oh Unborn Primeval Person, was dispelled by Your presence. What cold, darkness and fear would have power over someone who approached the sun?

(334) You who are so merciful in Your goodness offered to me Your servant, in return the torchlight consisting of Your wisdom. Whoever filled with gratitude can abandon the basis of Your feet and look for another shelter?

(335) The because of Your māyā firmly binding rope of my affection for the Dāśārhas, Vṛṣṇis, Andhakas and Sātvatas, cast by You for the production of offspring, was severed by the sword of the correct knowledge about the soul.

(336) Let me offer my obeisances unto You, oh Greatest Yogi, please tell me how I as a surrendered soul can be steadfast in the attraction of Your lotus feet.'

(337-340) The Supreme Lord said: 'Please Uddhava, accept My advice to head for My hermitage called Badārika. At the riverbanks there be purified by the touching of and bathing in the water emanating from My feet. Be, with your eyes fixed upon the Alakanandā [a tributary of the Ganges] cleansed of all impurities, dress yourself in bark My dear, eat from the forest and be happy freed from desire. Exercise with your intelligence, spiritual knowledge and wisdom, forbearance with all dualities, keep saintly to your principles, restrict your senses and live in peace and absorption. Believe in and meditate upon that what you from Me have learned to discriminate. When you with your words and mind absorbed in Me thus devote yourself to My dharma you will, with that discipline reaching beyond the three destinations [the guṇas or the three worlds], thereupon reach Me.'

(341) Śrī Śuka said: 'After thus having been addressed by the Lord of Understanding, Uddhava circumambulated Him keeping Him to the right and even though he at the time of his departure was free from the influence of material opposites, he with a breaking heart with his head bowed down flooded His feet with his teardrops.

(342) Finding it most difficult to let go of His love, he because of the departure was overwhelmed by emotions and could not abandon Him. Filled with pain he again and again offered his obeisances and placed the slippers of his Maintainer on his head. Then he departed [*].

(343) The great devotee then installed Him permanently in his heart and went to the illustrious place of pilgrimage [which as such is also called Viśālā] the One Friend in the Universe had mentioned. There properly executing his austerities, he attained the Lord's destination [Vaikuṇṭha].

(344) Anyone who with honest belief is full of attention for [listens to, speaks about and practices] this ocean of ecstasy, this nectarean sea of spiritual knowledge [of bhakti-yoga] that by Kṛishṇa, He whose feet are served by the masters of Yoga, was collected for His devotee, will liberate [himself and therewith] the entire world.

(345) I am bowed down to the greatest and first of all beings, the personality named Kṛiṣhṇa, who makes His many devotees drink the nectar from the [milk] ocean that is de essence of the Vedas, the essence of the spiritual knowledge and wisdom that He, as the author of the Vedas, like a bee delivered in order to take away the fear of material existence.*: The parampara adds here: 'According to the Śrīmad Bhāgavatam , while Uddhava was enroute to Badarikāśrama he heard about the Lord's journey to Prabhāsa. Turning back and following Lord Kṛṣṇa from behind, he saw the Lord alone just after the withdrawal of the Yadu dynasty. After being again mercifully instructed by the Personality of Godhead (along with Maitreya, who had just arrived), Uddhava felt his knowledge of the truth reawaken, and then, by the order of the Lord, he went on his way.'